Emerson Lake & Palmer

Greatest Hits

Order No. AM 934494
US International Standard Book Number: 0.8256.1536.4
UK International Standard Book Number: 0.7119.5421.6

Exclusive Distributors:
Music Sales Corporation
257 Park Avenue South, New York, NY 10010 USA
Music Sales Limited
8/9 Frith Street, London W1V 5TZ England
Music Sales Pty. Limited
120 Rothschild Avenue, Rosebery, NSW 2018, Australia

Printed in the United States of America by
Vicks Lithograph and Printing Corporation

Contents

C'est La Vie

by Greg Lake and Peter Sinfield

Moderately

8

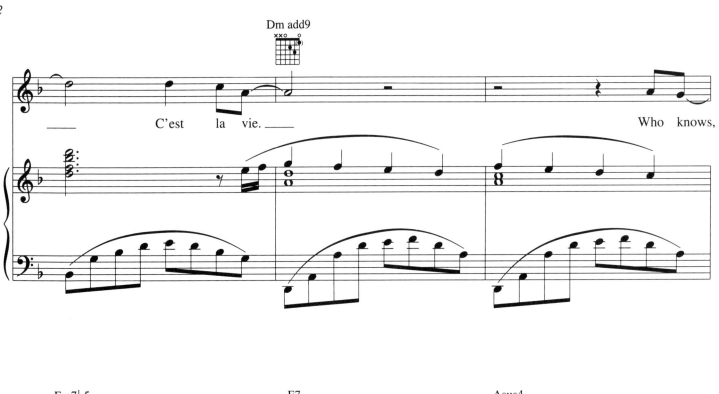

C'est la vie. ____ Who knows,

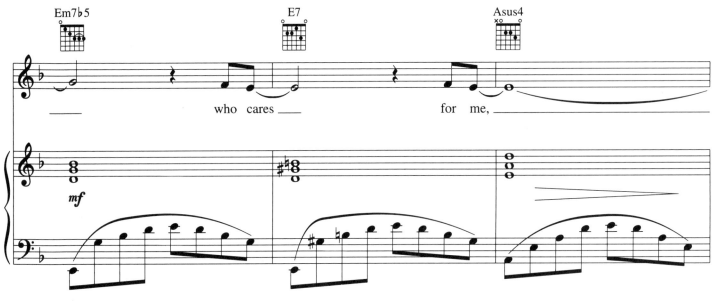

who cares ____ for me, ____

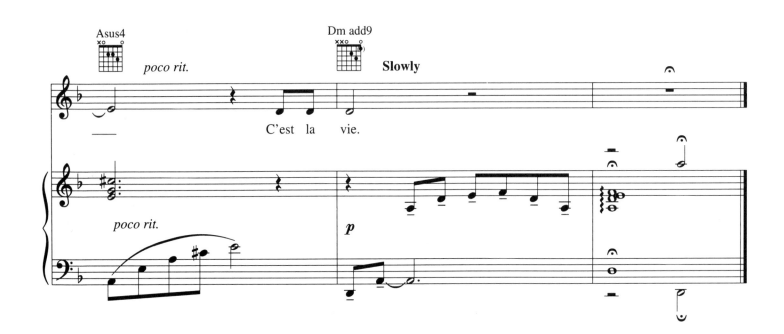

C'est la vie.

Still…You Turn Me On

BY GREG LAKE

The Endless Enigma Part I

by Keith Emerson and Greg Lake

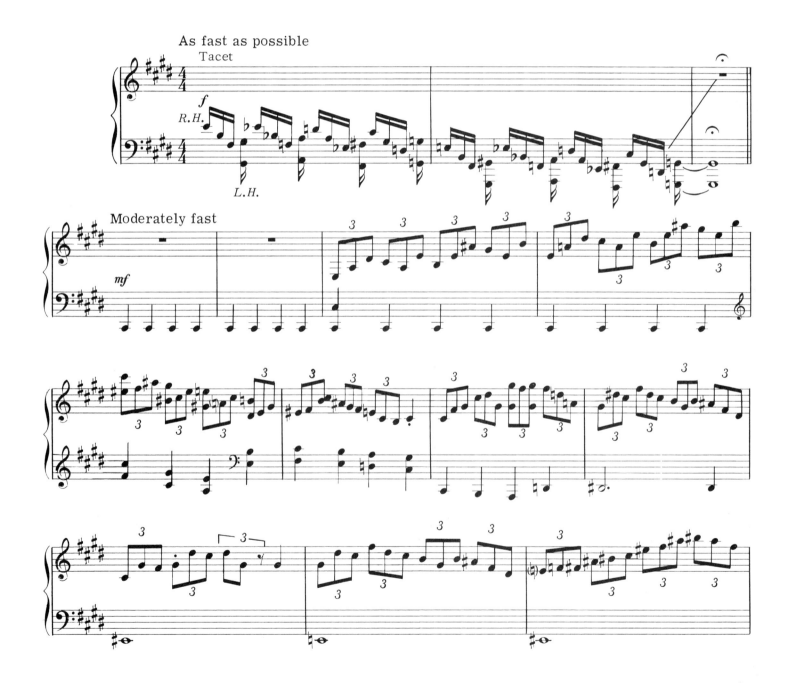

earth, wit-nessed my birth, cried at the sight of a man,
kings, pup-pets on strings dance for the chil-dren who stare;

and still I don't know who I am.
you must have seen them ev-'ry-where.

Tempo I
No chord

Repeat ad lib.
gradual cresc.

R.H.

ff

The Endless Enigma Part II

BY KEITH EMERSON AND GREG LAKE

From The Beginning

BY GREG LAKE

Take A Pebble

BY GREG LAKE

Moderately slow

* A cross (+) indicates that the key is to be depressed so that the hammer does not strike the strings. The strings are then to be plucked with a plectrum from inside the piano. (Do not depress the damper pedal, or all strings plucked will sound.)

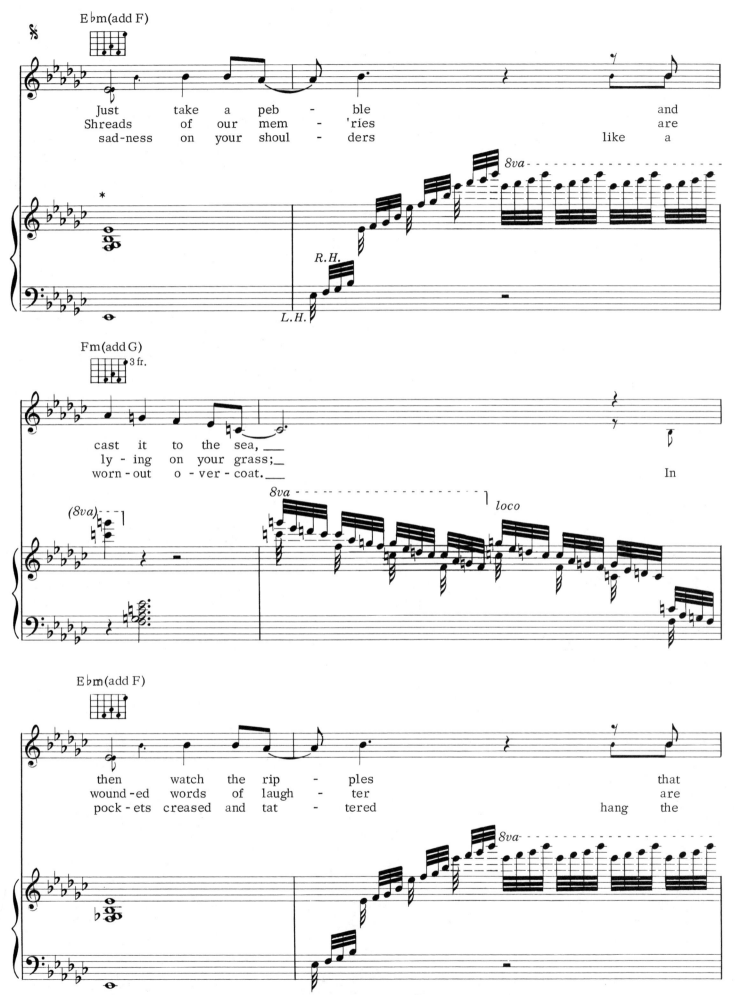

*First time play written accompaniment; second and third times improvise around written accompaniment.

lives. _____

are not real. _____

No chord

38

* Tune 6th string down one whole step to D.
Tune 3rd string up one whole step to A. (D A D A B E)

Improvise ad lib over left hand pattern.

I Believe In Father Christmas

BY GREG LAKE, PETER SINFIELD AND SERGE PROKOFIEFF

1. They said __ there'll be snow at Christ - mas. They said __ there'll be
2. They sold __ me a dream of Christ - mas. They sold __ me a

*Excerpt from LIEUTENANT KIJE by Prokofieff included by permission of the
Copyright Owners Boosey & Hawkes Music Publishers*

Christ-mas tree smell, ___ And their eyes full of tin - sel and fire. ___
first light of dawn, ___ And I saw him and through his dis - guise. ___

Excerpt from "Lieutenant Kijé" by Prokofieff included by permission of the Copyright Owners Boosey & Hawkes Music Publishers.

3. I wish you a hopeful Christmas
   I wish you a brave New Year
   All anguish, pain and sadness
   Leave your heart and let your road be clear.
   They said there'd be snow at Christmas
   They said there'd be peace on earth
   Hallelujah Noel be it heaven or hell
   The Christmas we get we deserve.

Lucky Man

BY GREG LAKE

Moderately slow

1. He _____ had white hors - es and la - dies _____ by the
2. White _____ lace and feath - ers they made up _____ his
3. *Instrumental solo*

score. ___ a All _____ dressed in sat - in and
bed, ___ a gold _____ cov - ered mat - tress on

Trilogy

BY KEITH EMERSON AND GREG LAKE

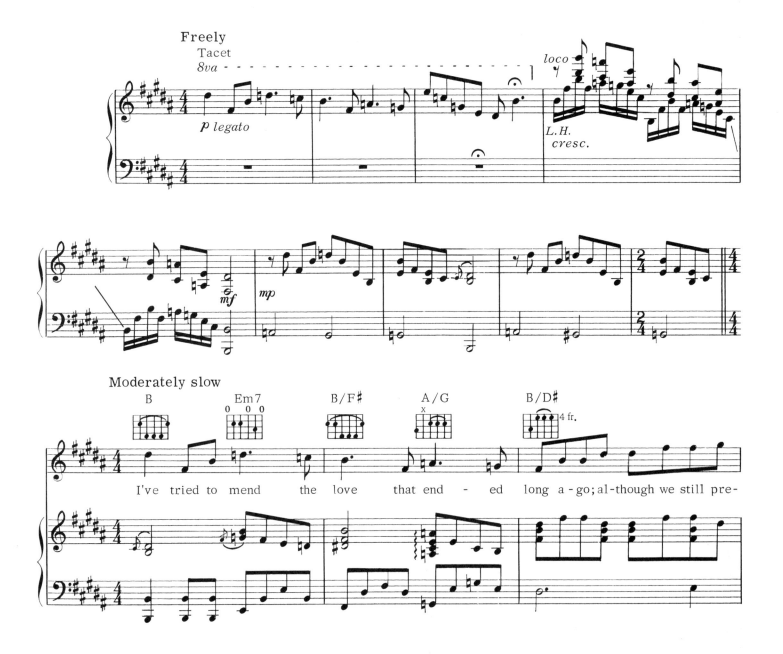

Double time feeling

Moderately, with a strong beat

We'll talk__ of plac - es that__ we went   and times that we   have
You'll see__ the day   an - oth - er   way   and wake   up with   the
You'll love__ a - gain,   I don't__ know when,   but if   you do   I

spent to - geth - er pen - ni - less and   free.
sun - shine pour - in' right down where you   lay.
know that you'll be hap - py   in the   end.

To Coda ⊕ |1.

* Play extended improvisation based on Bb7+9 chord before returning to 𝄋 .

Karn Evil 9 (1st Impression Part II)

BY KEITH EMERSON AND GREG LAKE

Bright rock

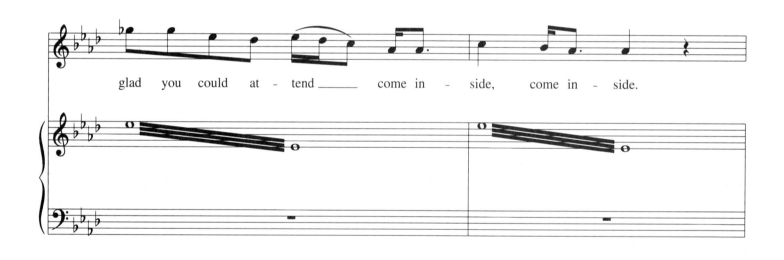

Come and see the show! ___ Come and see the show! ___ Come and see the

show! _____